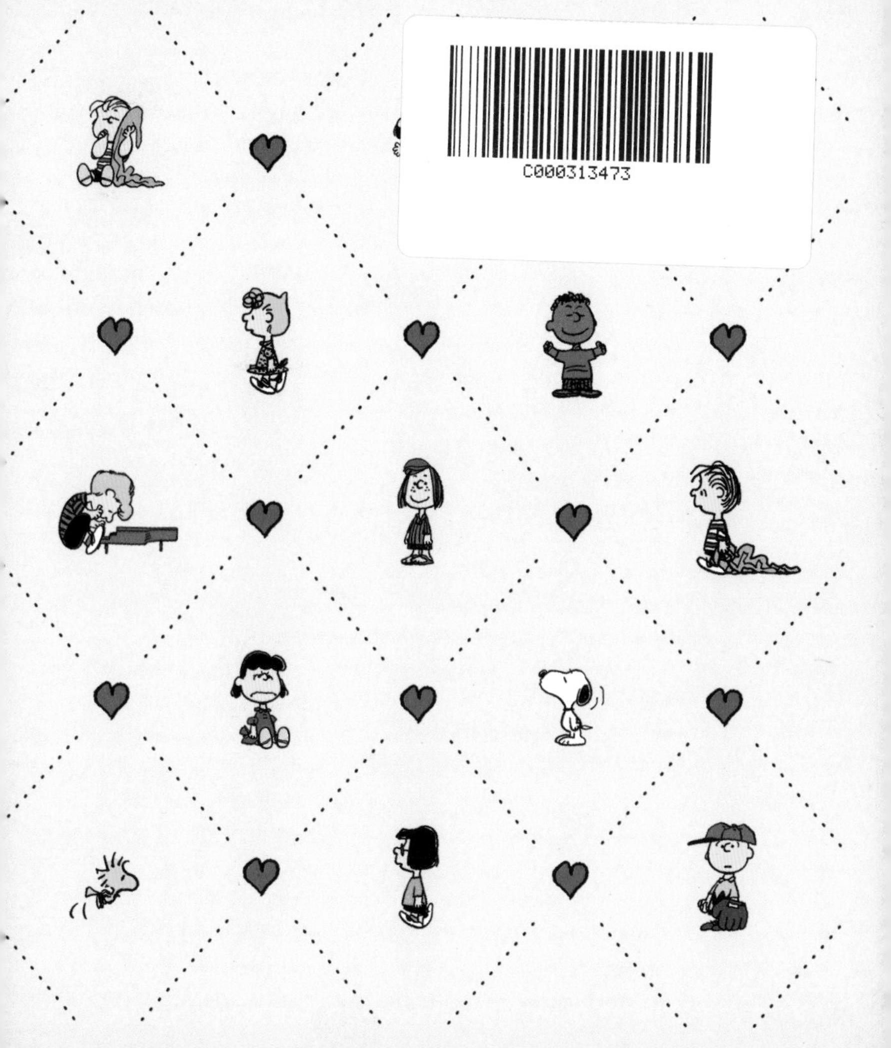

Published in Great Britain in 2015 by Canongate Books Ltd,
14 High Street, Edinburgh EH1 1TE

www.canongate.tv

1

British Library Cataloguing-in-Publication Data
A catalogue record for this book is available on
request from the British Library

ISBN 978 1 78211 373 7

PEANUTS written and drawn by Charles M. Schulz
Edited by Jenny Lord and Andy Miller
Design: Rafaela Romaya
Layout: Stuart Polson

Printed in China by C&C Offset Printing Co, Ltd

THE PEANUTS GUIDE TO
LOVE

CANONGATE

Edinburgh · London

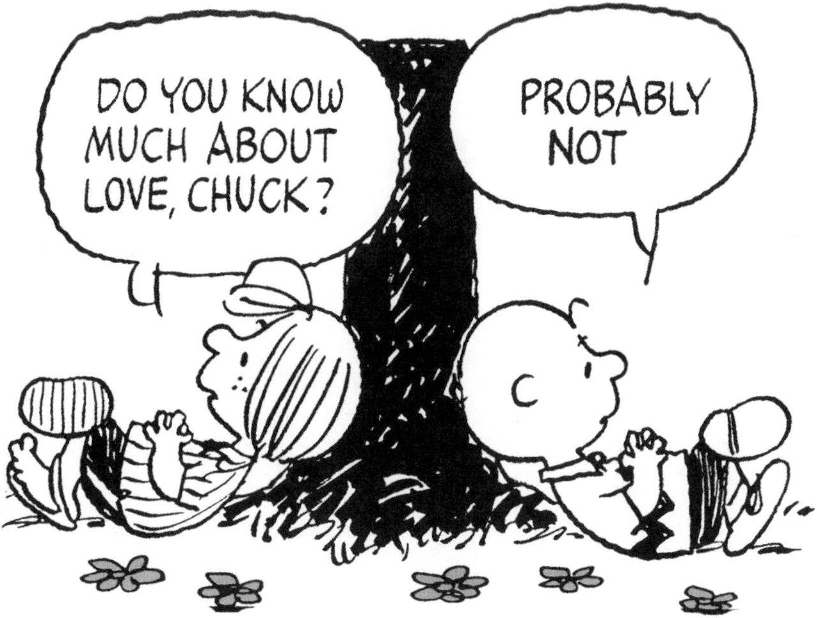
DO YOU KNOW MUCH ABOUT LOVE, CHUCK?
PROBABLY NOT

Dear Sweetheart,
I miss you
morning, noon
and night.
THAT'S
TOO
VAGUE..

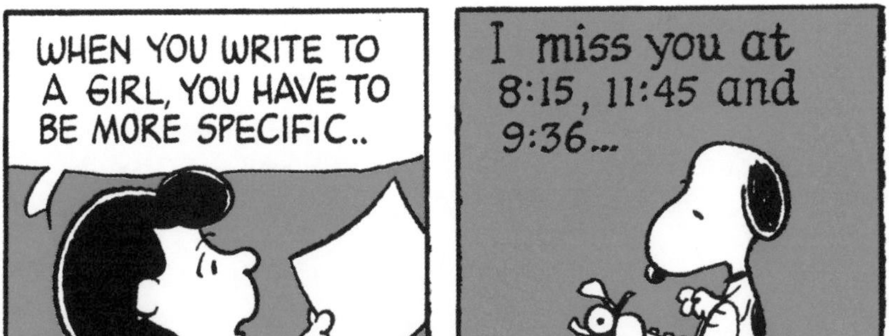
WHEN YOU WRITE TO A GIRL, YOU HAVE TO BE MORE SPECIFIC..
I miss you at 8:15, 11:45 and 9:36...

THIS IS PERFECT
I'LL JUST LIE HERE IN FRONT OF OUR MAILBOX AND WATCH ALL OF MY VALENTINES COME IN..

I'M SURPRISED THAT NO ONE ELSE HAS THOUGHT OF DOING THIS..

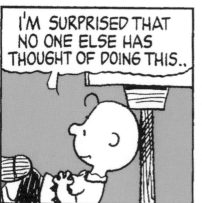

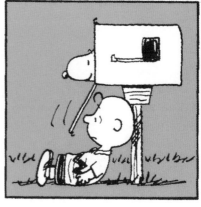

NEVER FALL IN LOVE WITH A MUSICIAN

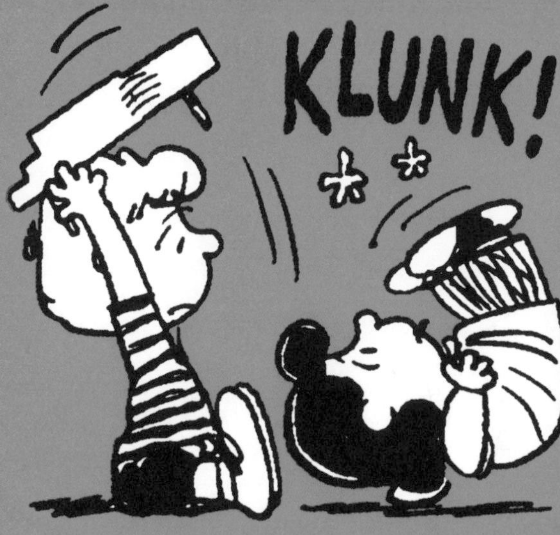
KLUNK!

I FALL IN LOVE TOO EASY..

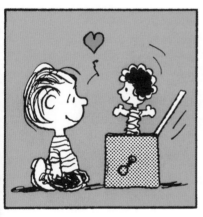

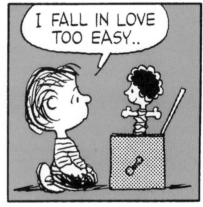

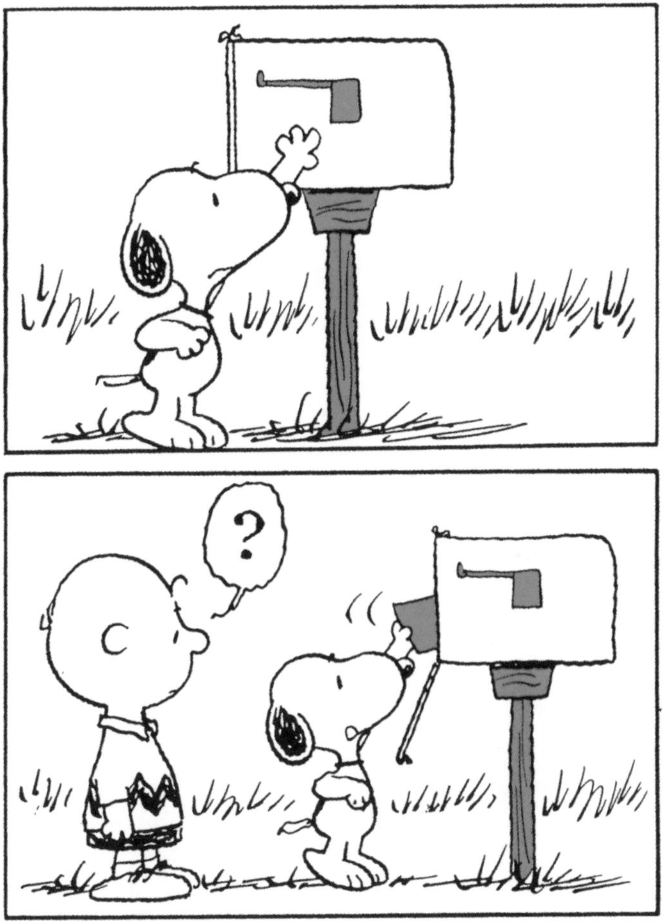
?

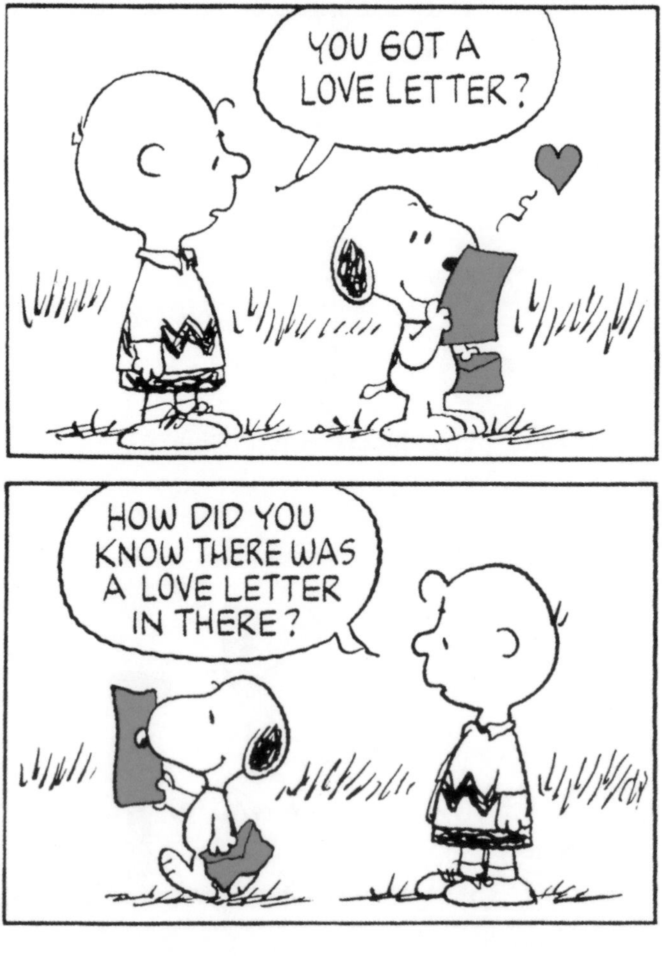
YOU GOT A LOVE LETTER?
HOW DID YOU KNOW THERE WAS A LOVE LETTER IN THERE?

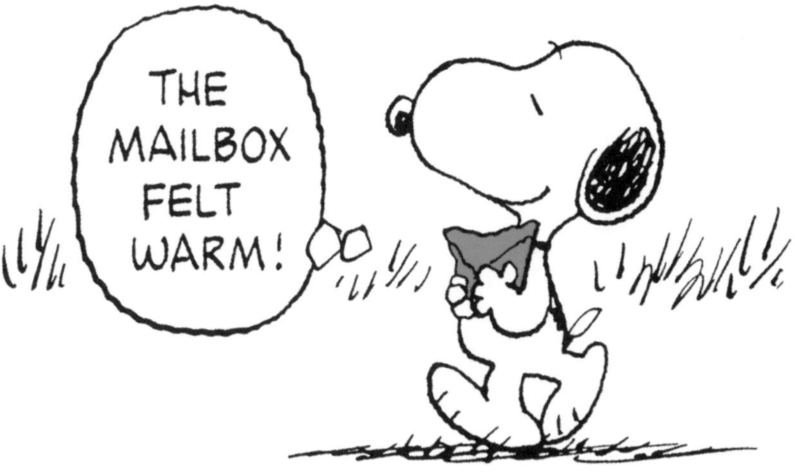
THE MAILBOX FELT WARM!

SEE THE VALENTINE I MADE FOR LINUS?
ON THE INSIDE I WROTE, "TO MY SWEET BABBOO"

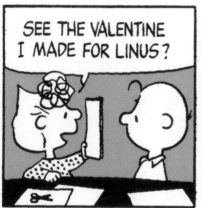

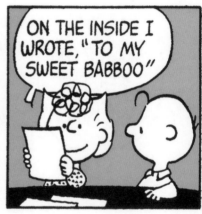

HE SAYS HE'S NOT YOUR "SWEET BABBOO"
WHAT DOES HE KNOW?

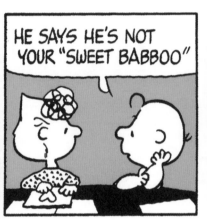

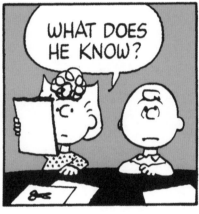

IT'S EITHER
FLU OR LOVE ...
THE SYMPTOMS
ARE THE SAME

MARCIE! WHAT ARE YOU DOING HERE?
I WANT YOU TO TAKE OFF THAT STUPID COSTUME, CHARLES, AND STOP LETTING YOURSELF BE HUMILIATED!

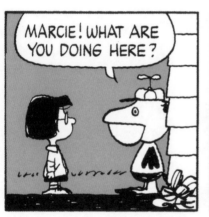

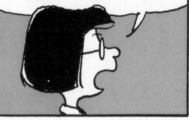

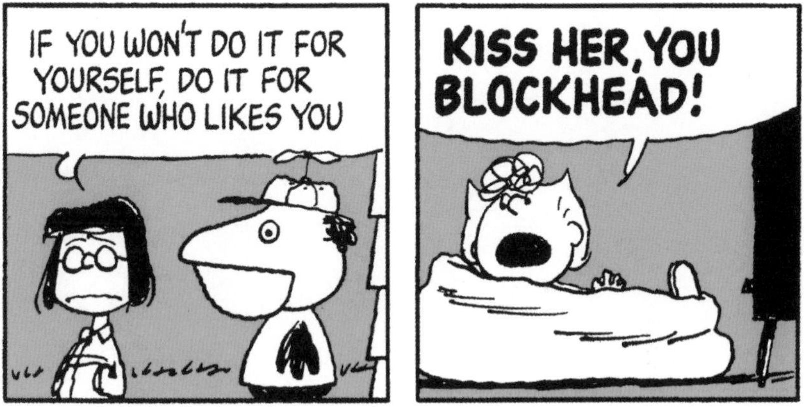
IF YOU WON'T DO IT FOR YOURSELF, DO IT FOR SOMEONE WHO LIKES YOU
KISS HER, YOU BLOCKHEAD!

Dear Sweetheart,
Without you my
days are endless.
Days seem like
weeks...weeks like
months...

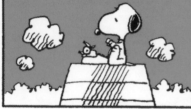

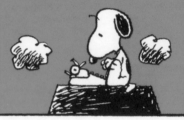

Months like years...
Years like centuries..
Centuries like...
You get the idea.

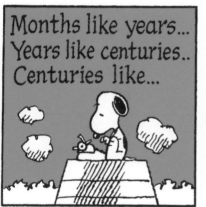

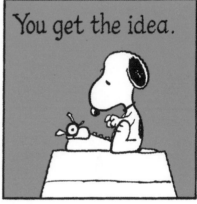

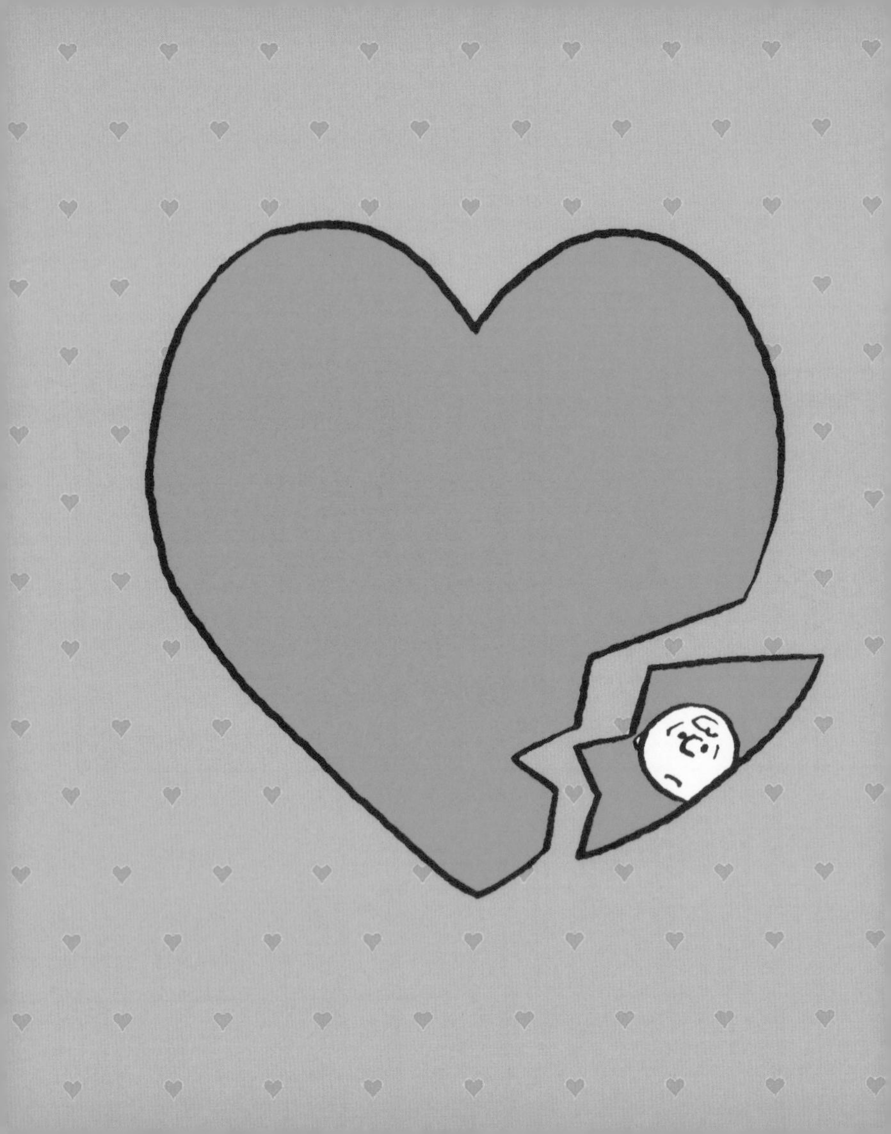

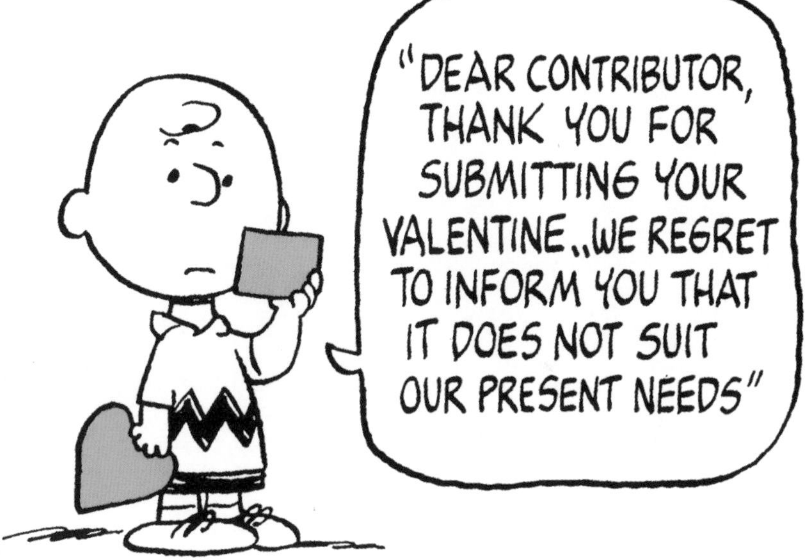
"DEAR CONTRIBUTOR, THANK YOU FOR SUBMITTING YOUR VALENTINE..WE REGRET TO INFORM YOU THAT IT DOES NOT SUIT OUR PRESENT NEEDS"

YOU KNOW WHAT SURPRISES ME?
I'M SURPRISED THAT YOU DIDN'T FALL IN LOVE WITH ME THE VERY FIRST TIME YOU SAW ME...

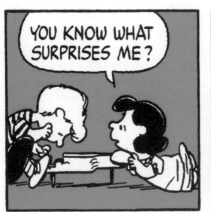

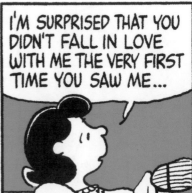

LIFE IS FULL OF SURPRISES

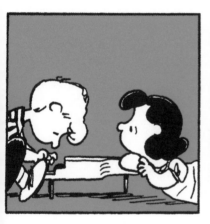

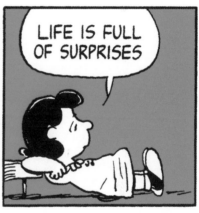

NOTHING TAKES THE TASTE OUT OF PEANUT BUTTER LIKE UNREQUITED LOVE!

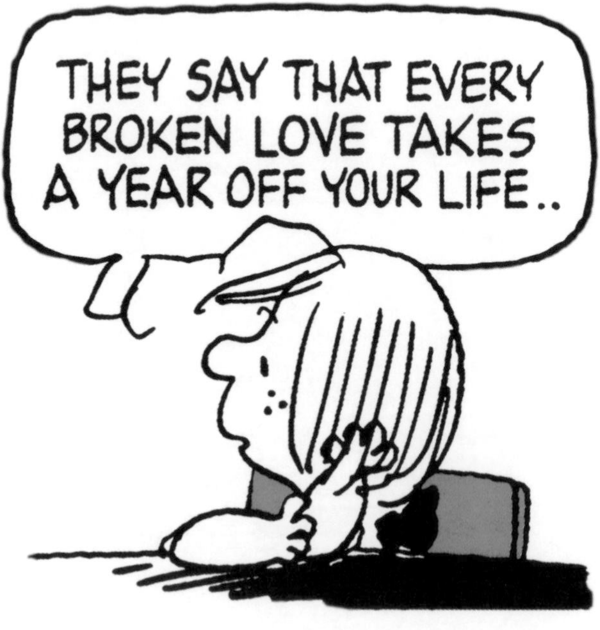
THEY SAY THAT EVERY BROKEN LOVE TAKES A YEAR OFF YOUR LIFE..

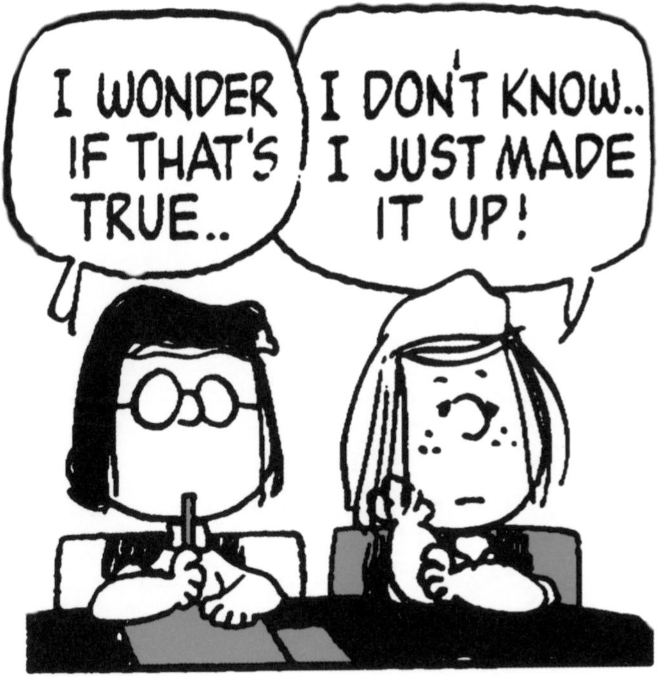
I WONDER IF THAT'S TRUE..
I DON'T KNOW.. I JUST MADE IT UP!

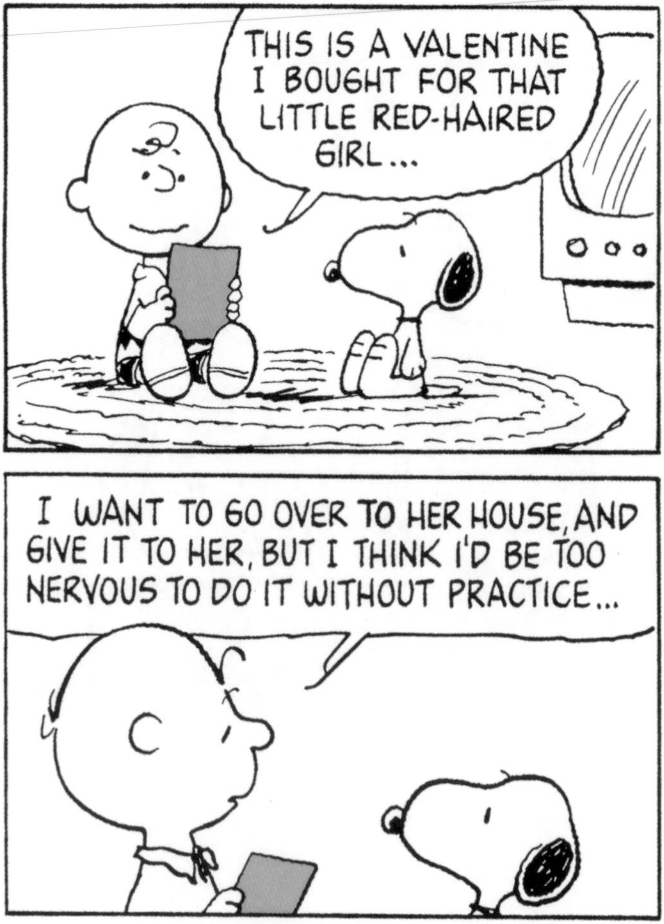
THIS IS A VALENTINE I BOUGHT FOR THAT LITTLE RED-HAIRED GIRL...
I WANT TO GO OVER TO HER HOUSE, AND GIVE IT TO HER, BUT I THINK I'D BE TOO NERVOUS TO DO IT WITHOUT PRACTICE...

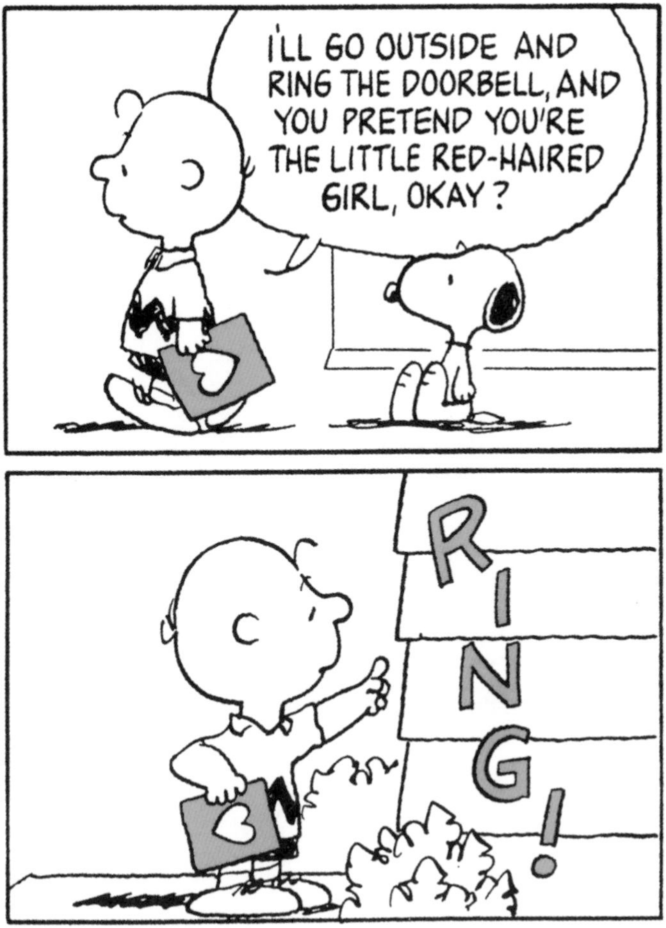
I'LL GO OUTSIDE AND RING THE DOORBELL, AND YOU PRETEND YOU'RE THE LITTLE RED-HAIRED GIRL, OKAY?
RING!

THIS IS OUR CLASS PICTURE... THERE'S PHIL, THE BOY I TOLD YOU ABOUT WHO LOVES ME
AND THAT'S SAMMY, WHO LOVES ME, AND FRED, WHO LOVES ME, AND WILLIAM, WHO LOVES ME, AND...

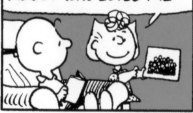

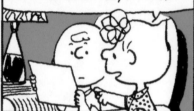

ALL THOSE BOYS LOVE YOU?
WHEN NO ONE LOVES YOU, YOU HAVE TO PRETEND THAT EVERYONE LOVES YOU!

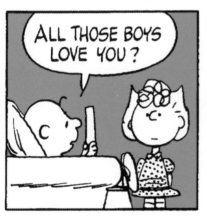

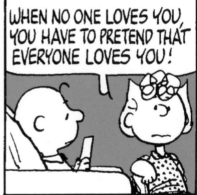

NEVER GIVE YOUR HEART TO A BLOCKHEAD

THERE'S THE HOUSE WHERE THE LITTLE RED HAIRED GIRL LIVES..
MAYBE IF I STAND HERE LONG ENOUGH, SHE'LL COME OUT...

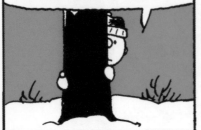

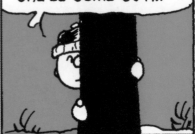

SHE DOESN'T KNOW THAT I COULD STAND HERE FOR HOURS..
I HAVE TO BECAUSE MY MITTENS ARE FROZEN TO THE TREE!

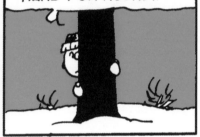

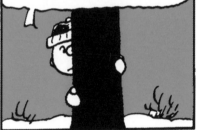

SOMETIMES LOVE
LETTERS GET STUCK
WAY IN THE BACK..

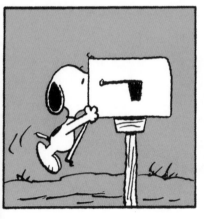

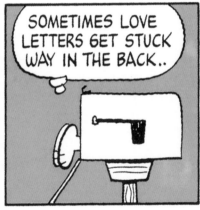

YOU'RE FOND OF ME?!
KISS HER, YOU BLOCKHEAD!

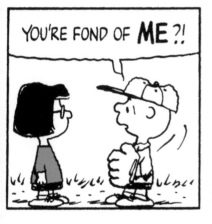

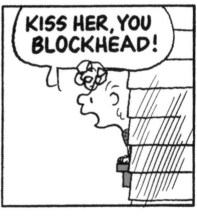

Dear Sweetheart,
I miss you
so much.
Tears of loneliness
fill my eyes as I
think of you.

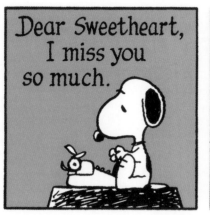

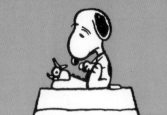

Tears of love drop onto these lines I write.
TEARS!

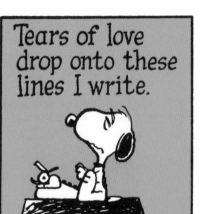

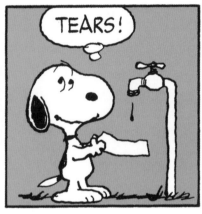

THE SECRET TO LOVE IS REMOVAL OF THE COMPETITION

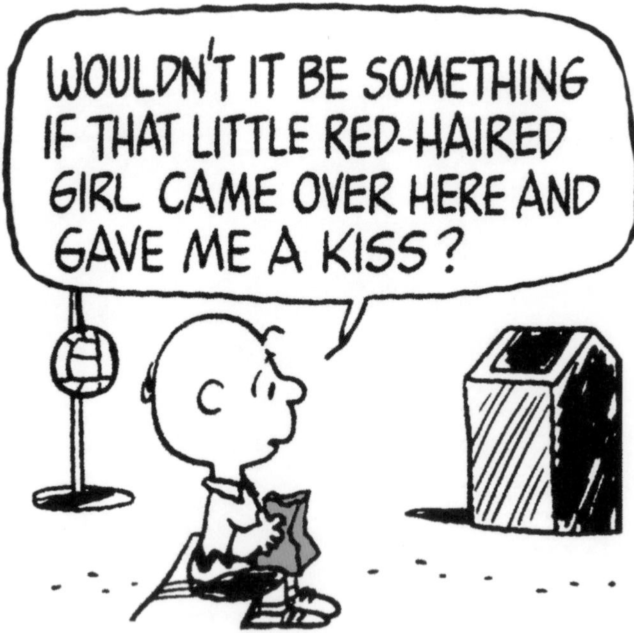
WOULDN'T IT BE SOMETHING IF THAT LITTLE RED-HAIRED GIRL CAME OVER HERE AND GAVE ME A KISS?

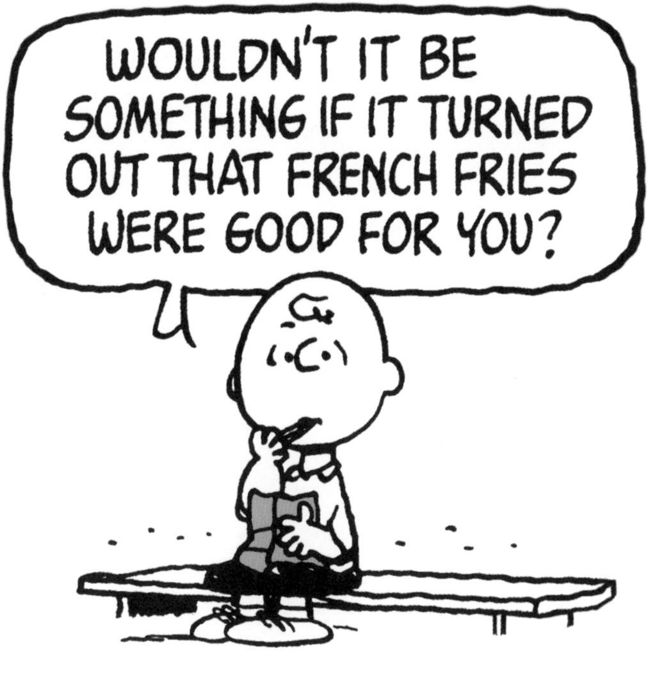
WOULDN'T IT BE SOMETHING IF IT TURNED OUT THAT FRENCH FRIES WERE GOOD FOR YOU?

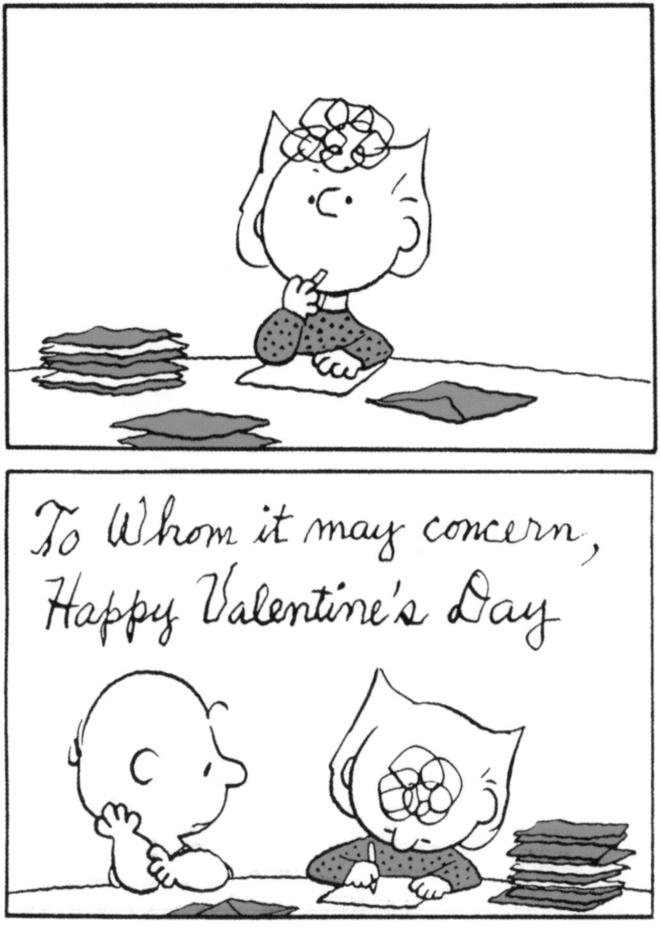
To Whom it may concern,
Happy Valentine's Day

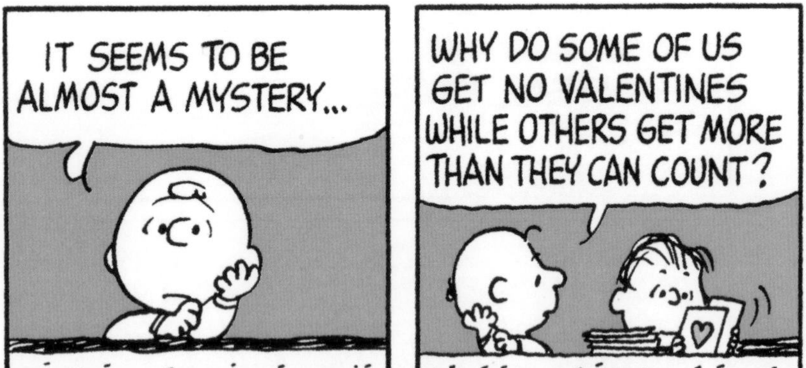
IT SEEMS TO BE ALMOST A MYSTERY...
WHY DO SOME OF US GET NO VALENTINES WHILE OTHERS GET MORE THAN THEY CAN COUNT?

YOU'RE RIGHT, CHARLIE BROWN...IT SEEMS TO BE A MYSTERY...
AND THOSE OF US WHO KNOW, WON'T TELL!

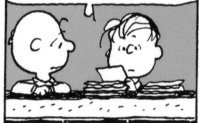

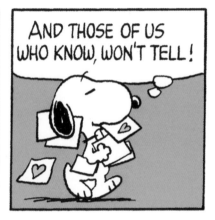

Dear Sweetheart,
Why did you
leave me?
Please come back.

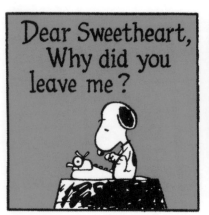

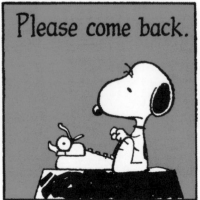

SUPPERTIME!
But not right now.

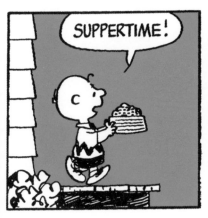

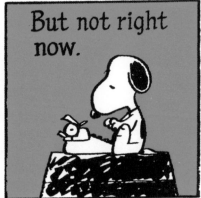

IT'S HARD TO LOVE SOMEONE WHO HITS YOU ON THE HEAD WITH A BASEBALL

ALL RIGHT, "AT EASE," OUT THERE! OUR TEACHER HAS ASKED ME TO EXPLAIN HOW THIS VALENTINE THING WILL WORK...
EACH STUDENT WILL DROP HIS OR HER VALENTINE INTO THIS BOX... PLEASE WRITE ALL NAMES CLEARLY...

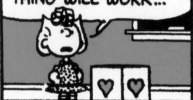

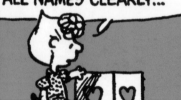

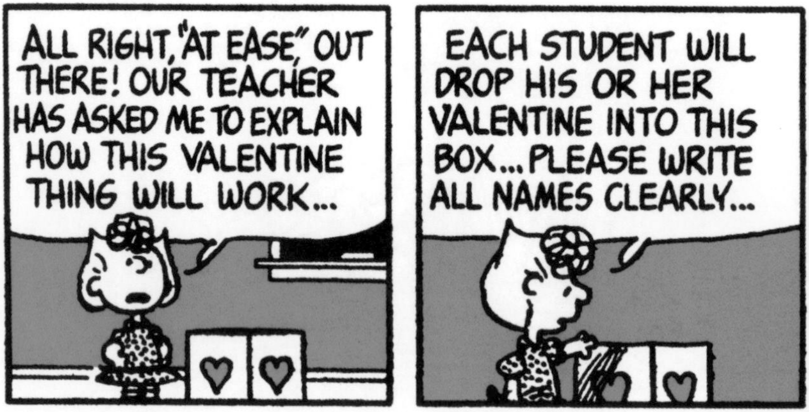

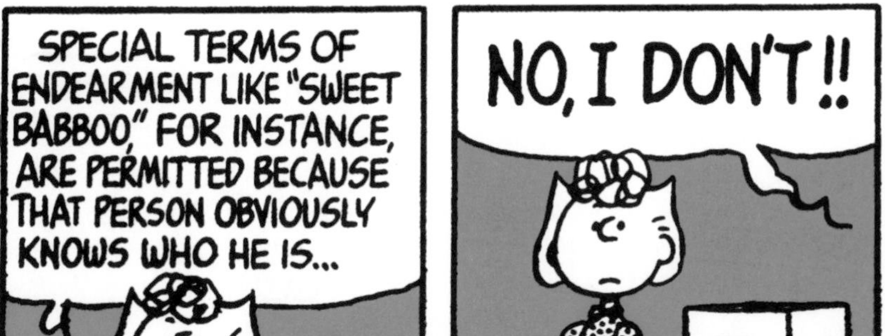
SPECIAL TERMS OF ENDEARMENT LIKE "SWEET BABBOO," FOR INSTANCE, ARE PERMITTED BECAUSE THAT PERSON OBVIOUSLY KNOWS WHO HE IS...
NO, I DON'T!!

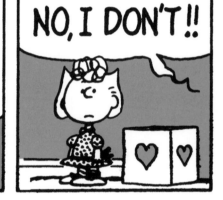

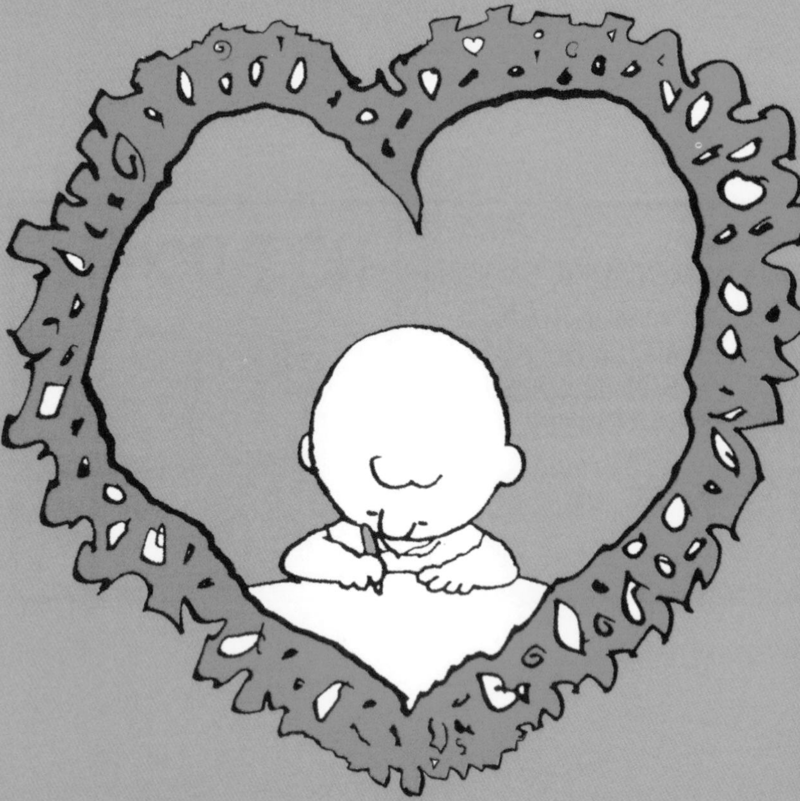

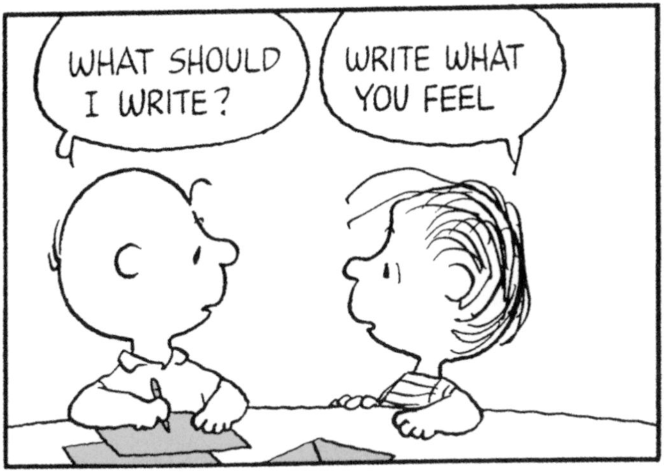
WHAT SHOULD I WRITE?
WRITE WHAT YOU FEEL

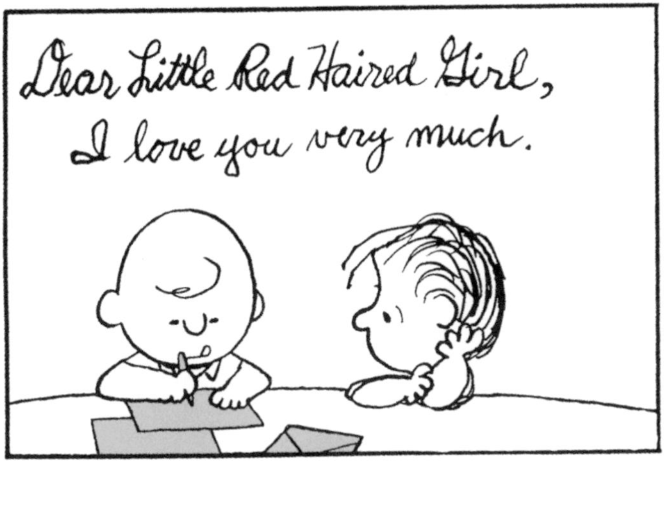
Dear Little Red Haired Girl,
I love you very much.

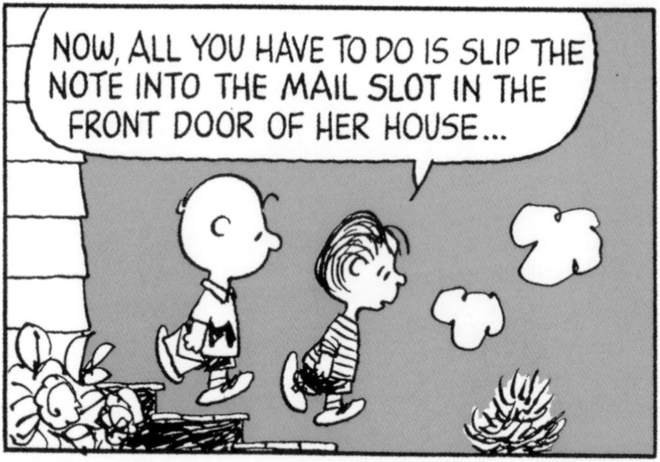
NOW, ALL YOU HAVE TO DO IS SLIP THE NOTE INTO THE MAIL SLOT IN THE FRONT DOOR OF HER HOUSE...

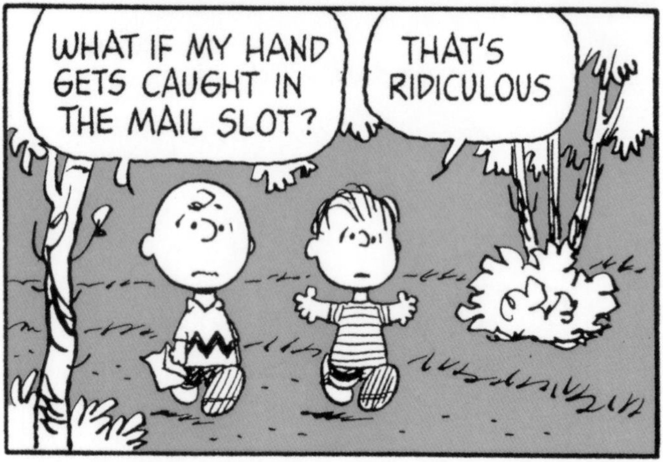
WHAT IF MY HAND GETS CAUGHT IN THE MAIL SLOT?
THAT'S RIDICULOUS

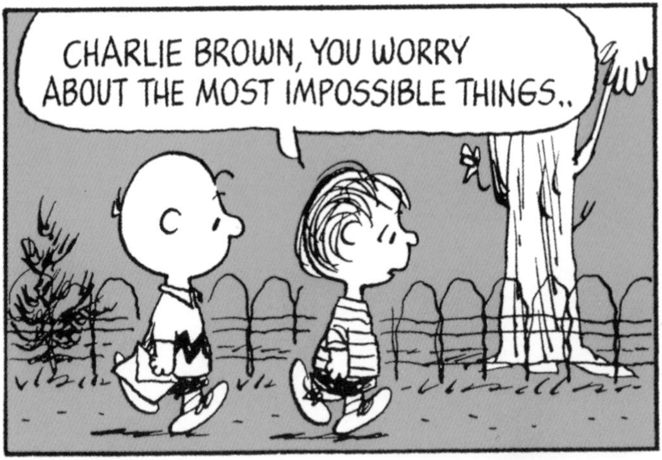
CHARLIE BROWN, YOU WORRY ABOUT THE MOST IMPOSSIBLE THINGS..

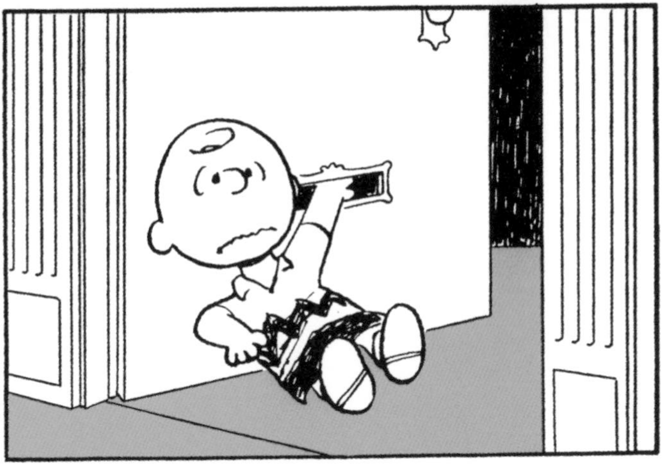

Dear Ex-Sweetheart, I still think of you often.
I loved you more than life itself, but you turned me down.

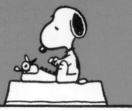

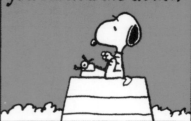

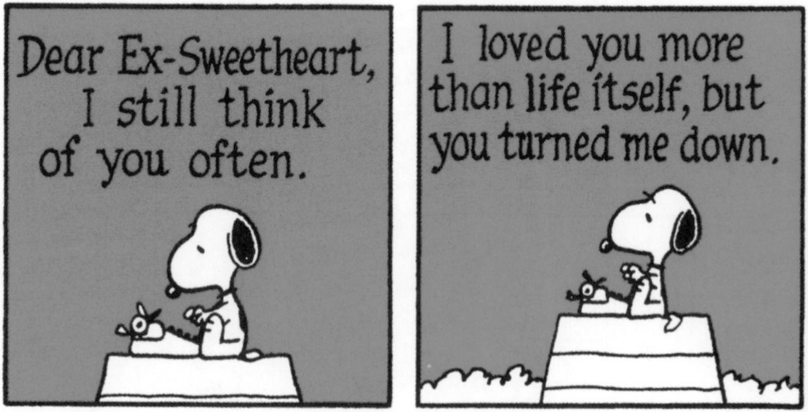

So why am I writing to you?
I'M NOT!

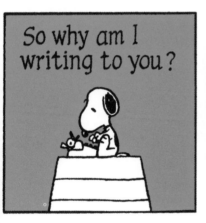

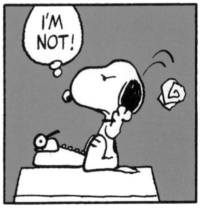

NEVER FALL
IN LOVE
WITH A
BUTTERFLY

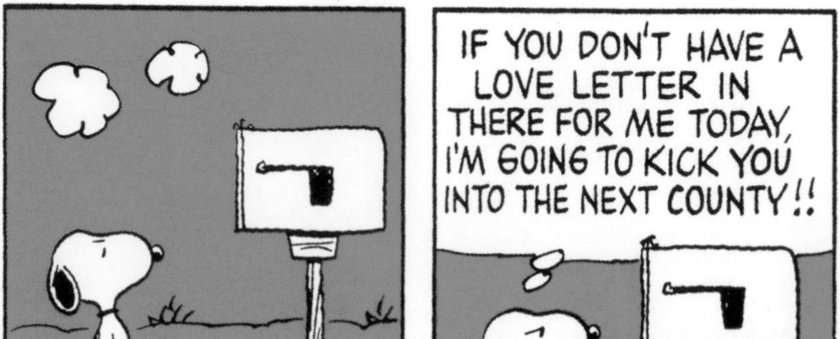
IF YOU DON'T HAVE A LOVE LETTER IN THERE FOR ME TODAY, I'M GOING TO KICK YOU INTO THE NEXT COUNTY!!

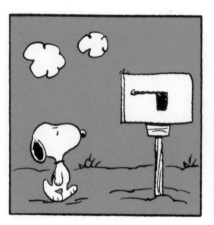

THAT'S THE ONLY KIND OF LANGUAGE A MAILBOX UNDERSTANDS!

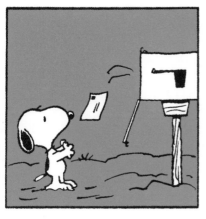

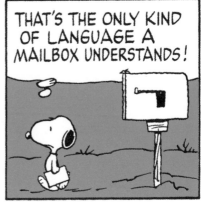

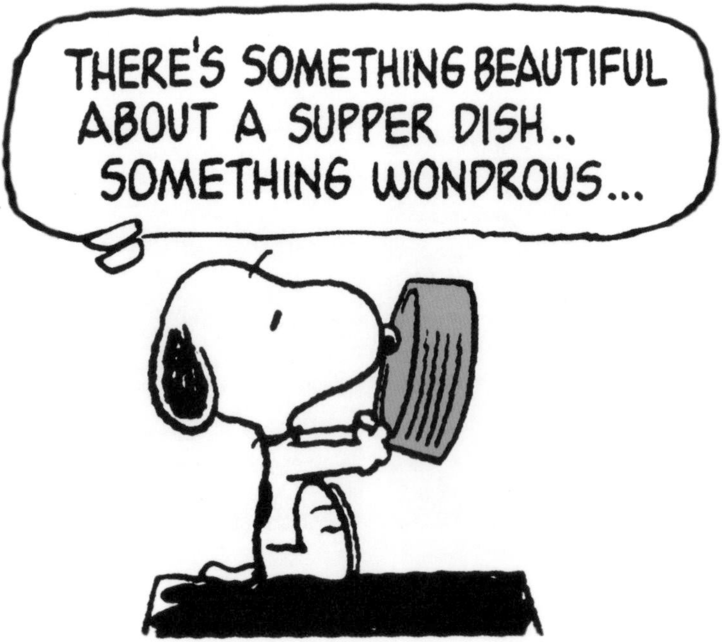
THERE'S SOMETHING BEAUTIFUL ABOUT A SUPPER DISH.. SOMETHING WONDROUS...

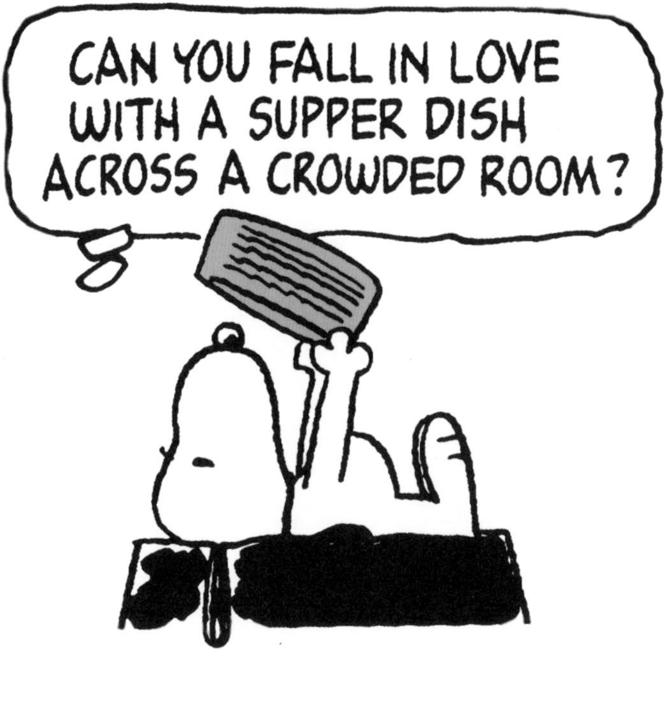
CAN YOU FALL IN LOVE
WITH A SUPPER DISH
ACROSS A CROWDED ROOM?

OKAY, GANG, IT'S TIME TO HEAD BACK HOME
WHO'S NOT GOING?

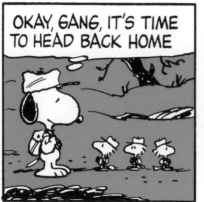

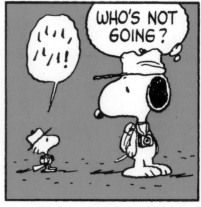

BILL AND HARRIET? WHY AREN'T THEY GOING? THEY'RE GETTING WHAT?
MARRIED?!!!

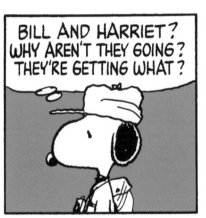

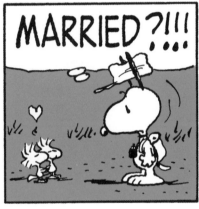

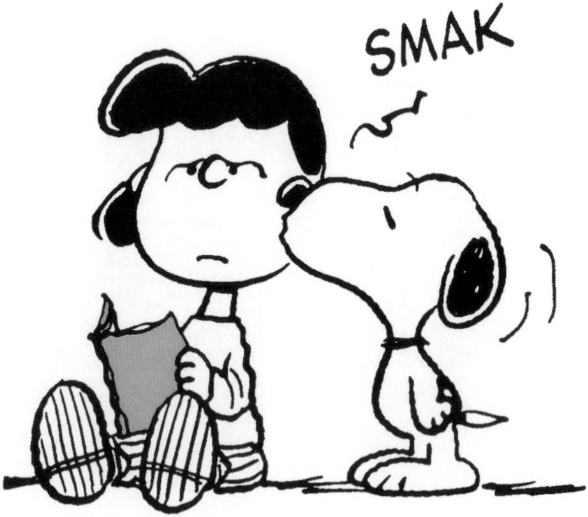
SMAK

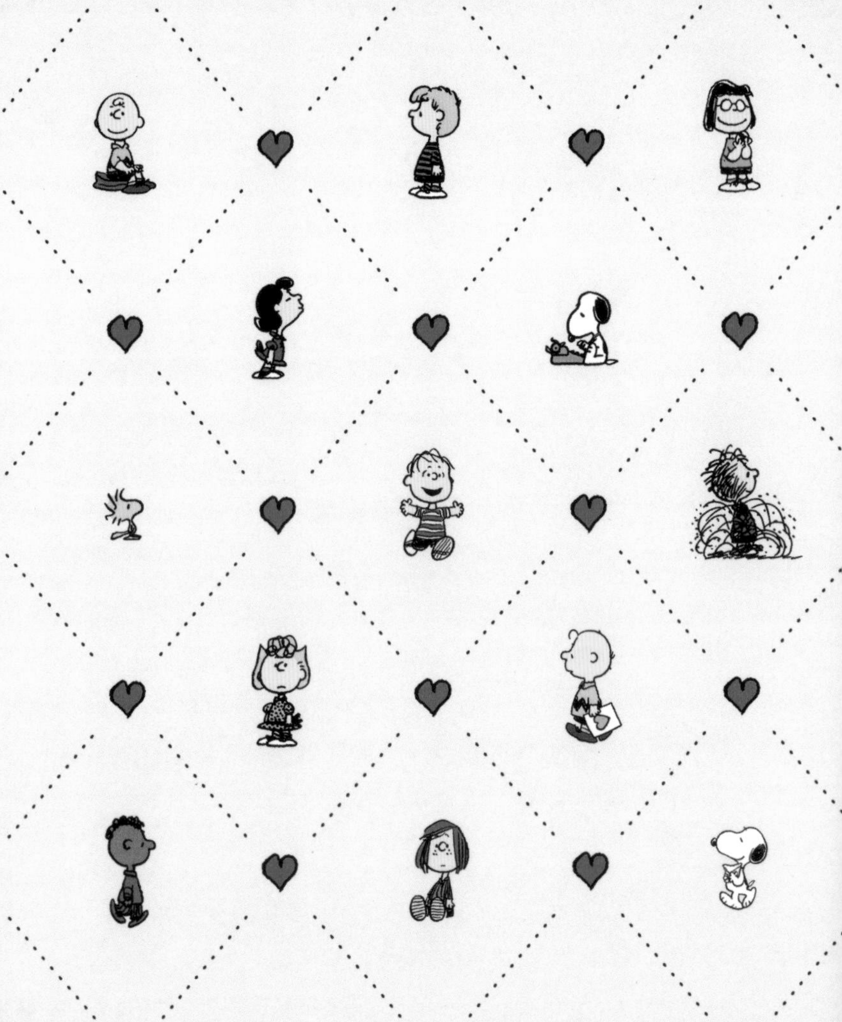